SCHOLAS

Now I Know My
NUMBERS
Learning Mats

50+ Double-Sided Activity Sheets That Help Children
Recognize, Write, and Count Numbers 1 to 30

Lucia Kemp Henry

New York • Toronto • London • Auckland • Sydney
Mexico City • New Delhi • Hong Kong • Buenos Aires

Teaching *Resources*

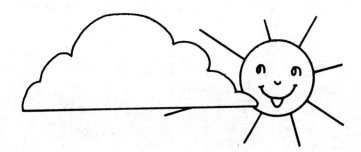

Edited by Immacula A. Rhodes
Cover design by Scott Davis
Interior illustrations by Lucia Kemp Henry
Interior design by Holly Grundon

ISBN: 978-0-545-32062-7

2 3 4 5 6 7 8 9 10   40   19 18 17 16 15 14 13

Contents

Learning Mats

Learning Mats (continued)

Mat	Skill
49–50	Identifying 20 and *twenty*; Counting to 20
51–52	Identifying 21 and *twenty-one*; Counting to 21
53–54	Identifying 22 and *twenty-two*; Counting to 22
55–56	Identifying 23 and *twenty-three*; Counting to 23
57–58	Identifying 24 and *twenty-four*; Counting to 24
59–60	Identifying 25 and *twenty-five*; Counting to 25
61–62	Identifying 26 and *twenty-six*; Counting to 26
63–64	Identifying 27 and *twenty-seven*; Counting to 27
65–66	Identifying 28 and *twenty-eight*; Counting to 28
67–68	Identifying 29 and *twenty-nine*; Counting to 29
69–70	Identifying 30 and *thirty*; Counting to 30
71–72	Identifying 40 and *forty*; Counting to 40
73–74	Identifying 50 and *fifty*; Counting to 50
75–76	Identifying 60 and *sixty*; Counting to 60
77–78	Identifying 70 and *seventy*; Counting to 70
79–80	Identifying 80 and *eighty*; Counting to 80
81–82	Identifying 90 and *ninety*; Counting to 90
83–84	Identifying 100 and *one hundred*; Counting to 100
85–86	Identifying Even Numbers
87–88	Identifying Odd Numbers
89–90	Counting Practice to 12 and to 15
91–92	Counting Practice to 28 and to 30
93–94	Counting Practice to 60 and to 100
95–96	Comparing Sets: More
97–98	Comparing Sets: Fewer
99–100	Matching Numbers & Number Words
101–102	Matching Numbers & Number Words
103–104	Writing Numbers 1–50 and 51–100

About This Book

Welcome to *Now I Know My Numbers Learning Mats*! The 104 double-sided mats in this book provide engaging activities designed to help children master essential number recognition and counting skills. In addition, the systematic format reinforces literacy and fine-motor skills while enabling children to work independently.

The interactive, reproducible mats feature appealing art and simple, predictable text to target the numbers 1 to 30, increments of 10 up to 100, and other key number concepts. Activities include identifying, writing, and matching numbers and number words; counting; comparing quantities to numbers; creating and comparing sets; distinguishing between odd and even numbers; and sequencing. The drawing and writing exercises help develop and strengthen fine-motor skills as well as reinforce letter and word recognition. And, as children read and follow directions to complete each mat, they build critical vocabulary and comprehension skills. To help meet the learning needs of your students, refer to page 8 to see how activities in this book connect to the Common Core State Standards for Mathematics, Reading (Foundational Skills), and Language, as well as the standards recommended by the National Council of Teachers of Mathematics (NCTM).

Preparing and using the learning mats is quick and easy! Simply make double-sided copies to use for instruction with the whole class, small groups, student pairs, or individuals. The mats are also ideal for independent work, centers, and homework. You'll find that daily practice with these activities helps build and reinforce skills in number concepts and boosts early literacy skills. Best of all, children will experience the joy of learning as they develop skills that help them grow more confident in themselves as learners.

What's Inside

Each ready-to-go learning mat in this resource targets a specific number or number concept. To use, simply decide on the skill you want to teach, locate the corresponding mats in the book, and make a double-sided copy of the selected mats. The only materials kids need for the activities are crayons or colored pencils. To use, children read and follow the directions to preform each activity. You'll find several activity formats throughout the book, as described below:

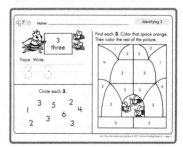

✤ **Trace the Number:** Children trace the number and then write it on their own without guides. This exercise reinforces number formation and helps build fine-motor skills.

✤ **Identify the Number:** Visual discrimination skills are reinforced as children distinguish the target number from an array of other numbers.

✤ **Hidden Picture:** Children identify the target number and color that space as directed to reveal a hidden picture or shape.

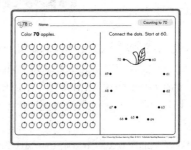

✤ **Count and Color:** Counting skills get a boost as children count out and color a specific number of items.

✤ **Drawing:** Develop fine-motor skills with this activity while reinforcing the targeted number concept.

✤ **Count the Sets:** This activity helps children make the connection between quantities and numbers in print.

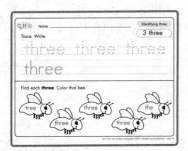

✤ **Trace the Word:** Reinforce word recognition, spelling, and letter formation as children trace the number word.

✤ **Identify the Word:** Children use visual discrimination skills to identify the target number word from similarly spelled or shaped words.

✤ **Color the Quantity:** Children color the specified number of items.

✤ **Connect-the-Dot Puzzles:** Build skills in counting higher numbers (from 30 to 100) with these simple connect-the-dot activities.

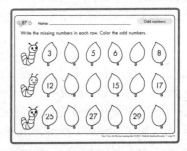

✤ **Odd or Even Number:** Children fill in the missing numbers and then color all of the odd or even numbers in the series.

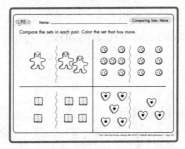

✤ **Compare Sets:** In this activity, children compare two sets to determine which has more or fewer items.

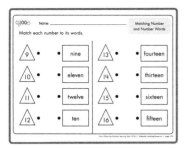

❖ **Match Numbers and Words:**
Children draw lines to match each number
to the correct number word.

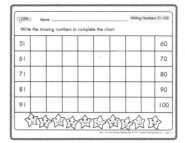

❖ **Number Chart:** As children write
numbers in the chart, they practice
sequencing and number formation.

Helpful Tips

The following suggestions will help you and your students get the most out of the learning mats:

- Complete each mat in advance to become familiar with the directions, art, and response for each activity. If desired, laminate your completed copy to use as an answer key. (Or slip the mat into a clear, plastic page protector.) You might bind all of your answer keys into a notebook to keep on hand for children to check their work.

- Use the mats to introduce new concepts, track children's progress in mastering essential skills, and review concepts already covered.

- Prepare the mats for repeated use in learning centers. Simply laminate the double-sided mats and put them in a center along with wipe-off color crayons and paper towels (to use as erasers).

- Compile sets of the learning mats into booklets for children to complete in class or at home. For example, you might staple copies of mats 1–6 between two sheets of construction paper and title the booklet, "My Book of Numbers: 1 and 2."

- The mats are also perfect for instant homework assignments. Send the pages home with children to complete. This is an easy way to reinforce skills covered in class as well as to help keep families informed about what their children are learning, what they've mastered, and where they might need some extra guidance.

Meeting the Standards

Connections to the Common Core State Standards

The Common Core State Standards Initiative (CCSSI) has outlined learning expectations in English/Language Arts and Mathematics for students at different grade levels. The activities in this book align with the following standards for students in grades K–1. For more information, visit the CCSSI Web site at www.corestandards.org.

Mathematics

Counting & Cardinality

- K.CC.1. Count to 100 by ones and by tens.

- K.CC.2. Count forward beginning from a given number within the known sequence.

- K.CC.3. Write numbers from 0 to 20. Represent a number of objects with a written numeral 0-20 (with 0 representing a count of no objects).

- K.CC.4. Understand the relationship between numbers and quantities; connect counting to cardinality.

- K.CC.5. Count to answer "how many?" questions; given a number from 1–20, count out that many objects.

- K.CC.6. Identify whether the number of objects in one group is greater than, less than, or equal to the number of objects in another group.

- K.CC.7. Compare two numbers between 1 and 10 presented as written numerals.

Reading Standards: Foundational Skills

Print Concepts

- RF.K.1, RF.1.1. Demonstrate understanding of the organization and basic features of print.

- RF.K.1a. Recognize and name all upper- and lowercase letters of the alphabet.

Phonological Awareness

- RF.K.2, RF.1.2. Demonstrate understanding of spoken words, syllables, and sounds (phonemes).

Phonics and Word Recognition

- RF.K.3, RF.1.3. Know and apply grade-level phonics and word analysis skills in decoding words.

Fluency

- RF.K.4, RF.1.4. Read with sufficient accuracy and fluency to support comprehension.

- RF.1.4a. Read grade-level text with purpose and understanding.

- RF.1.4b. Read grade-level text orally with accuracy, appropriate rate, and expression.

- RF.1.4c. Use context to confirm or self-correct word recognition and understanding, rereading as necessary.

Language

Conventions of Standard English

- L.K.1, L.1.1. Demonstrate command of the conventions of standard English grammar and usage when writing or speaking.

- L.K.1a, L.1.1a. Print upper- and lowercase letters.

- L.K.2, L.1.2. Demonstrate command of the conventions of standard English capitalization, punctuation, and spelling when writing.

Connections to the NCTM Math Standards

The activities in this book are also designed to support you in meeting the following PreK–1 standards—including process standards, such as problem solving, reasoning and proof, and communication—recommended by the National Council of Teachers of Mathematics (NCTM):

Understands numbers, ways of representing numbers, relationships among numbers, and number systems

- Counts with understanding and recognizes "how many" in sets of objects

- Develops understanding of the relative position and magnitude of whole numbers

- Connects number words and numerals to the quantities they represent

Source: National Council of Teachers of Mathematics. (2000). *Principles and Standards for School Mathematics.* Reston, VA: NCTM. www.nctm.org

Name: _____

☆ 1
☆☆

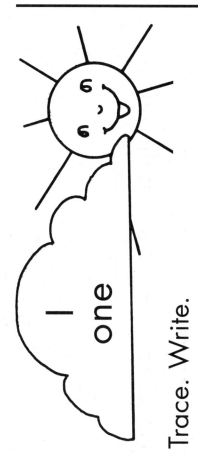

1
one

Trace. Write.

Find each **1**. Color that space yellow.
Then color the rest of the picture.

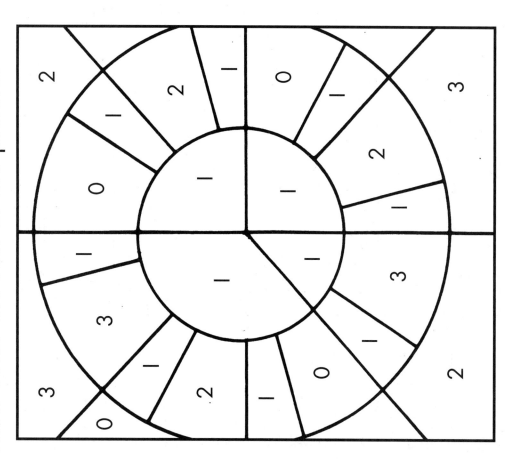

Circle each **1**.

2 3 0 1 0

1 3 2 1

Name: _____

Color 1 sun in each row.

1.

2.

3.

Draw 1 sun in the sky.

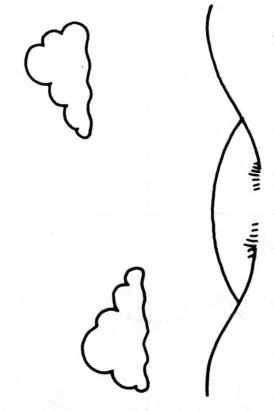

How many suns? Write the number in the box.

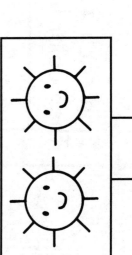
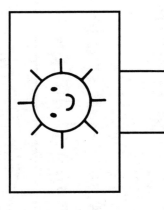
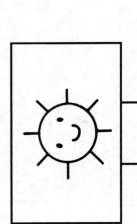

Find each **2.** Color that space brown.
Then color the rest of the picture.

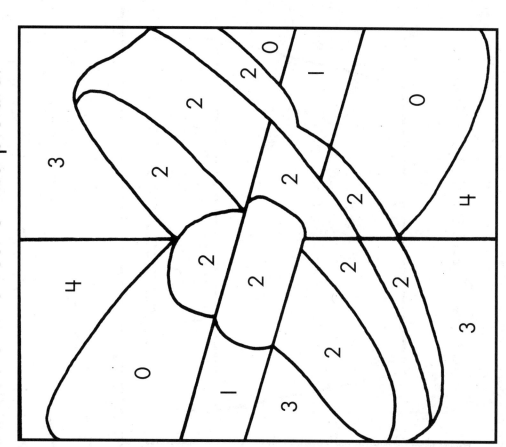

Name: _____

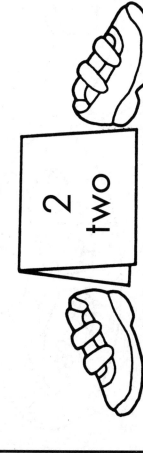

2
two

Trace. Write.

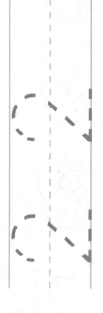

Circle each **2.**

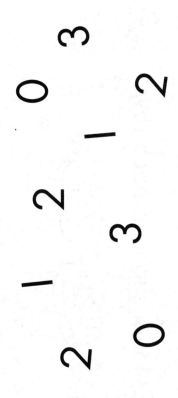

2   1   2   1   0   3

0   3   2

4

Name: _____

Color **2** shoes in each row.

1.

2.

3.

Draw **2** shoes in the box.

Shoes

How many shoes? Write the number in the circle.

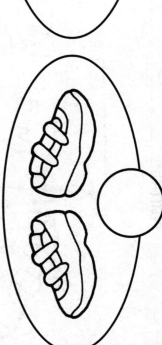

5 ⭐⭐⭐

Name: _____

I one

Trace. Write.

one one one

one

Find each **one**. Color that sun.

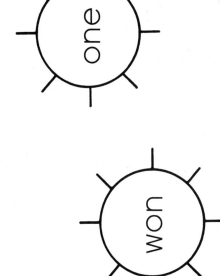 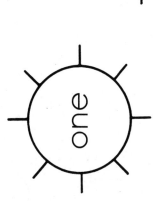 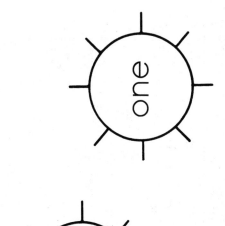

on   one   one   won   one

Name: _____

☆☆☆ 6

Trace. Write.

2 two

t-w-o t-w-o

two

Find each **two**. Color that shoe.

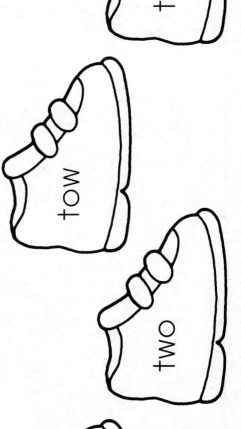

two   two   tow   two   ton

7 ☆☆☆

Name: _____

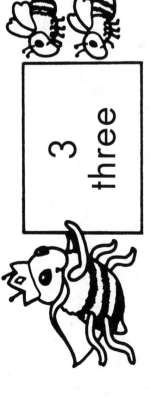

3
three

Trace. Write.

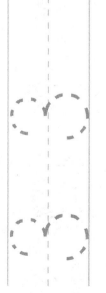

Circle each **3**.

1   3   5   2   4

2   3   6   3

Find each **3**. Color that space orange.
Then color the rest of the picture.

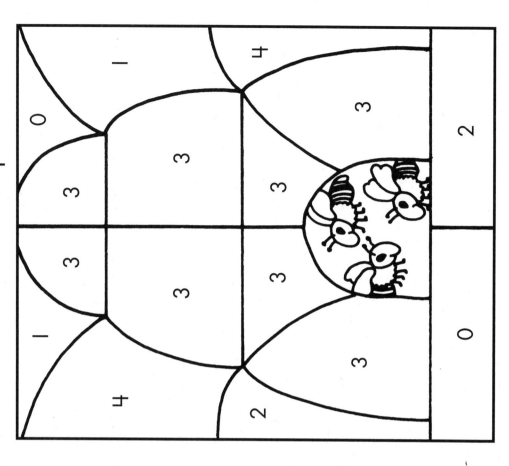

4		
1	3	3
3		0
3		1
3	3	4
3	3	
2	3	3
0	2	

⭐ 8 ⭐
☆ ☆

Name: _____

Color **3** bees in each row.

1.

2.

3.

Draw **3** bees on the flower.

How many bees? Write the number in the box.

 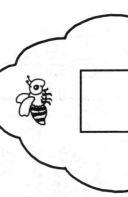 

Name: _____

⭐ 9

Find each **4**. Color that space green.
Then color the rest of the picture.

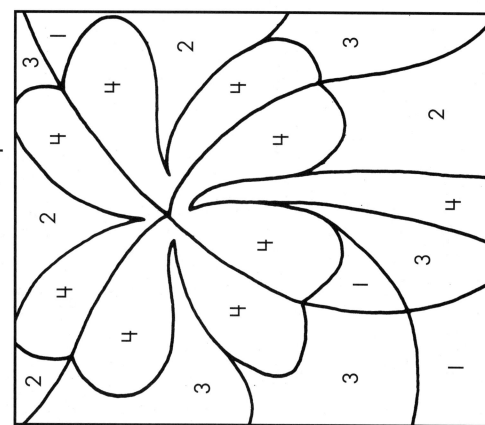

Trace. Write.

4
four

Circle each **4**.

1 4 2 3 1 4

3 4 2

Name: _____

10

Draw **4** ladybugs on the clover.

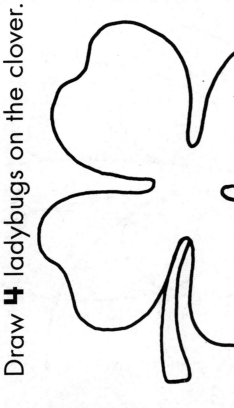

Color **4** clovers in each row.

1.

2.

3.

How many ladybugs? Write the number on the line.

 _____

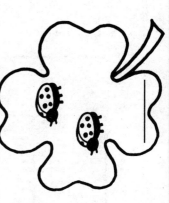 _____

 _____

Name: _____

Identifying three

3 three

Trace. Write.

three three three

three

Find each **three**. Color that bee.

the

three

three

three

tree

12 ☆☆☆

Name: _____

4 four

Trace. Write.

four four

four

Find each **four.** Color that clover.

for

four

four

fan

four

Find each **5**. Color that space yellow.
Then color the rest of the picture.

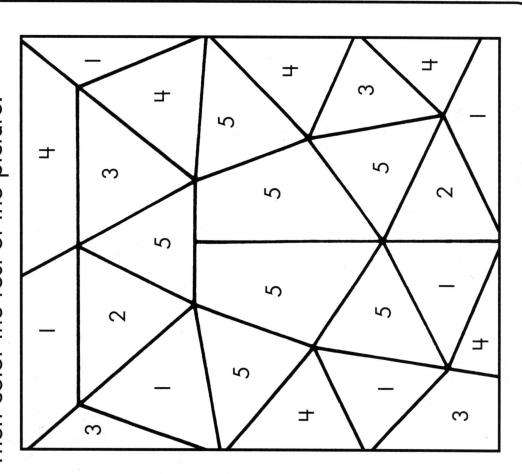

Name: _____

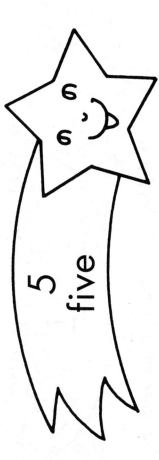

5
five

Trace. Write.

Circle each **5**.

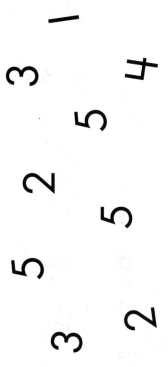

5   2   3   1

3   5   5   4

3   2

Name: _____

14

Color 5 stars in each row.

1. ☆ ☆ ☆ ☆ ☆ ☆

2. ☆ ☆ ☆ ☆ ☆

3. ☆ ☆ ☆ ☆ ☆ ☆

Draw 5 stars in the sky.

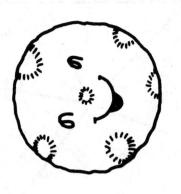

How many stars? Write the number in the circle.

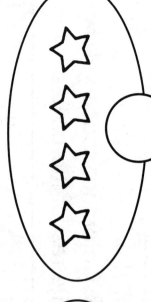

Name: _____

Find each **6**. Color that space yellow. Then color the rest of the picture.

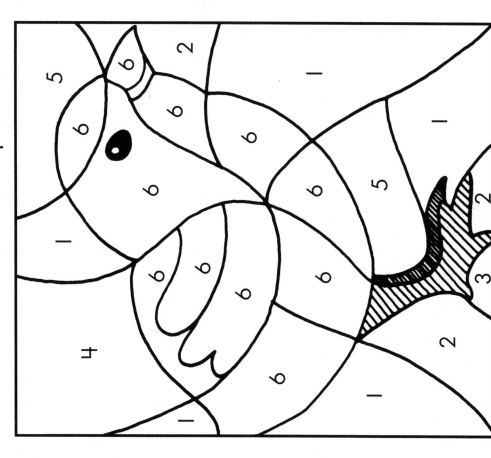

5

6

6

6

6

1

4

6

6

6

6

6

6

6

6

9

2

1

6

5

1

2

3

2

1

1

6
six

Trace. Write.

_____

Circle each **6**.

4   6   1   5

6   3   2   6

0

15

Draw **6** eggs in the nest.

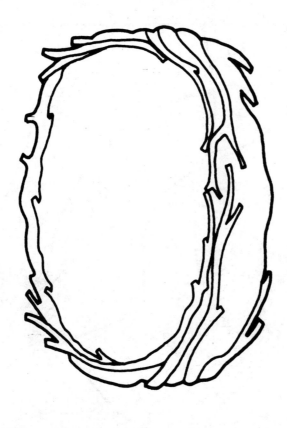

Name: _____

☆ 16 ☆

Color **6** chicks in each row.

1.

2.

3.

How many eggs? Write the number in the box.

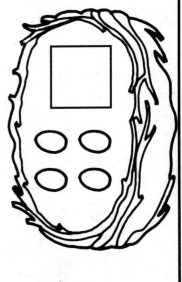

17 ☆
☆☆

Name: _____

5 five

Trace. Write.

five

five

five

Find each **five**. Color that star.

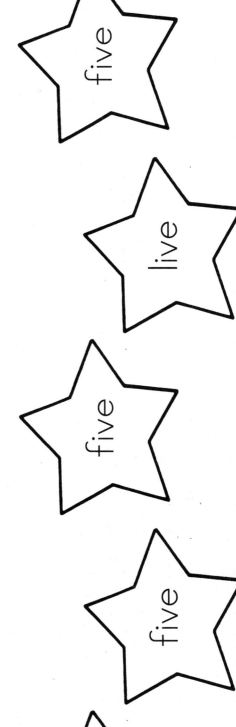

fire

five

five

live

five

☆☆

Name: _____

6 six

Trace. Write.

six six six

six six six

six

Find each six. Color that chick.

sit

six

six

exit

six

Find each **7**. Color that space red.
Then color the rest of the picture.

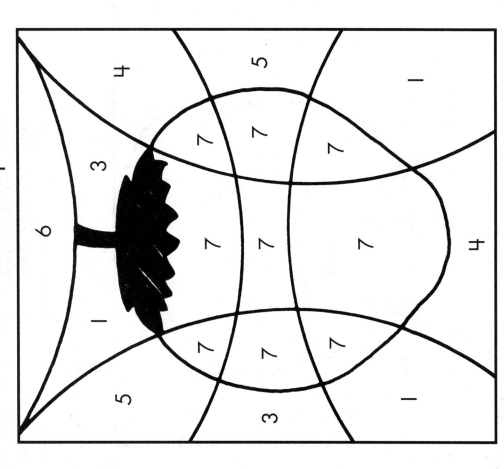

Name: _____

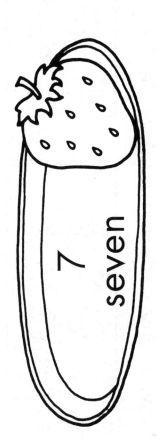

7

seven

Trace. Write.

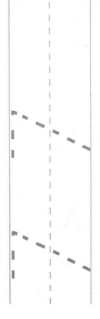

Circle each **7**.

6   5   2   1   3   7

7   7   4

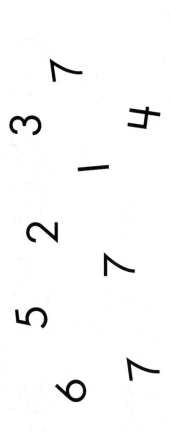

Name: _____

Color **7** strawberries.

Draw **7** seeds on the strawberry.

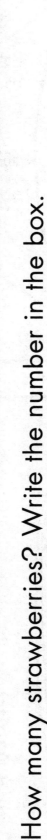

How many strawberries? Write the number in the box.

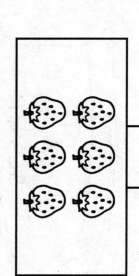
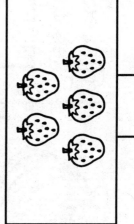
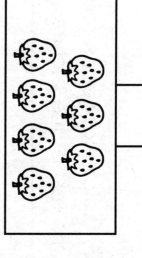

Name: _____

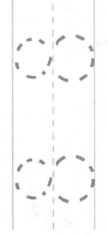

8
eight

Find each 8. Color that space pink.
Then color the rest of the picture.

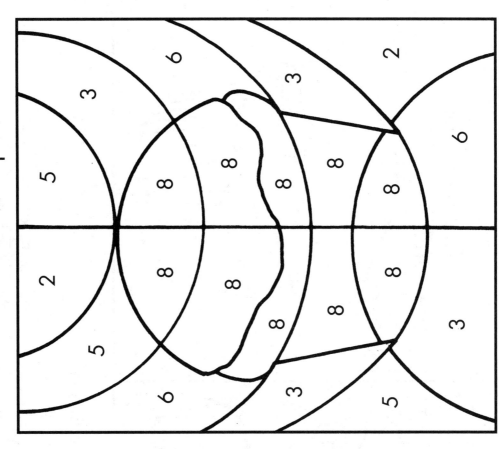

Trace. Write.

Circle each 8.

3   8   6   5   3   8

4   8   8   5   2

Name: _____

Color **8** cupcakes.

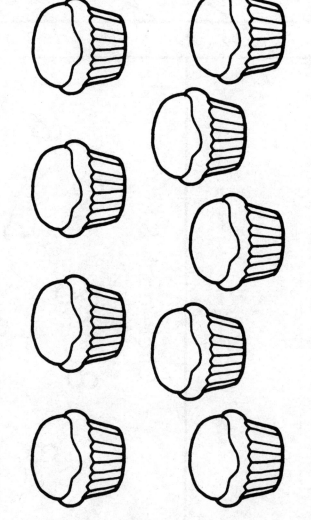

Draw **8** candies on the cupcake.

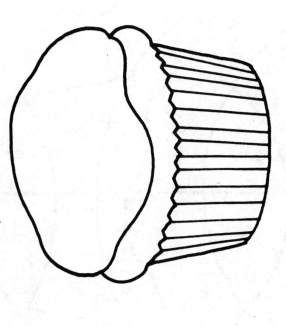

How many candies? Write the number on the line.

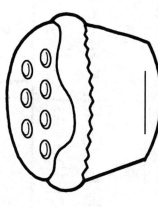

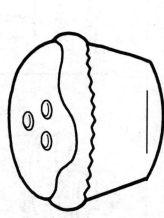

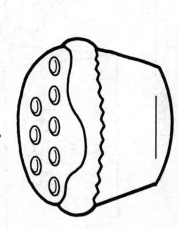

☆ **23** ☆
☆

Name: _____

7 seven

Trace. Write.

seven seven

seven

Find each **seven**. Color that strawberry.

seven

even

sent

seven

seven

Name: _____

Identifying eight

8 eight

Trace. Write.

eight

eight

Find each **eight**. Color that cupcake.

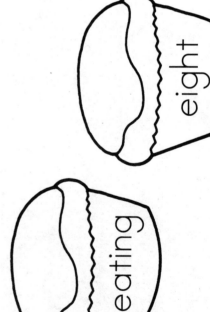

eight

eating

eight

sight

eight

Find each **9**. Color that space brown.
Then color the rest of the picture.

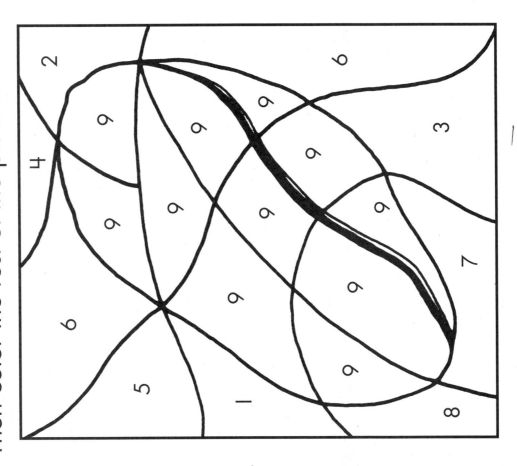

Name: _____

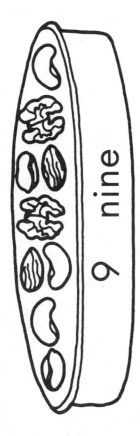

9 nine

Trace. Write.

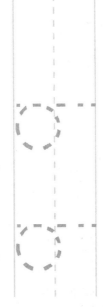

Circle each **9**.

0 6 9 6
4 9 3
7 9
9

25

26

Name: _____

Color **9** nuts.

Draw **9** nuts in the hand.

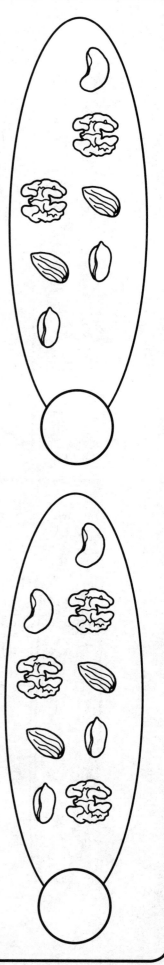

How many nuts? Write the number in the circle.

Name: _____

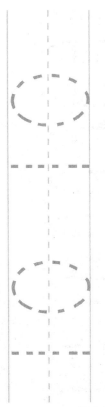

10
ten

Trace. Write.

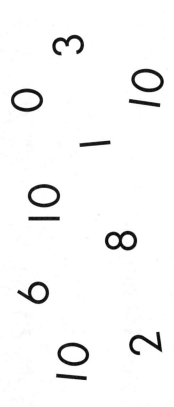

Circle each **10**.

10   6   10   0   3

2   8   I   10

Find each **10**. Color that space blue.
Then color the rest of the picture.

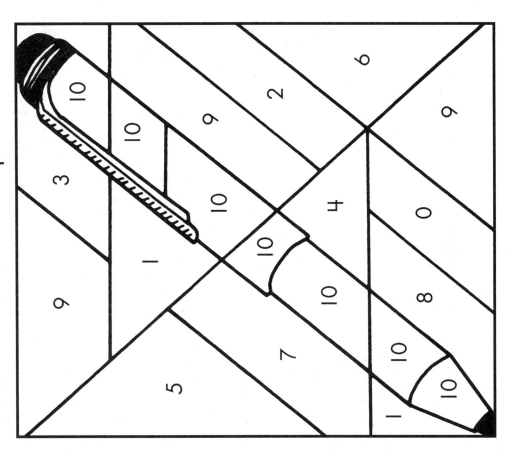

27

Name: _____

☆28☆

Color **10** pens.

Draw **10** pens in the box.

Pens

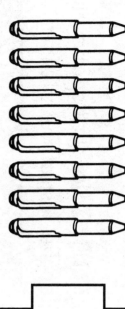

How many pens? Write the number in the box.

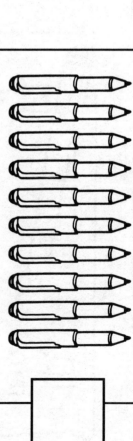

Name: _____

9 nine

Trace. Write.

nine nine nine

nine

Find each **nine**. Color that nut.

nine

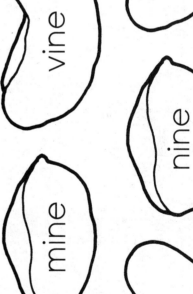

nine

vine

nine

mine

nine

wine

☆30 ☆☆

Name: _____

Trace. Write.

ten ten ten

ten ten

ten

Find each **ten**. Color that pen.

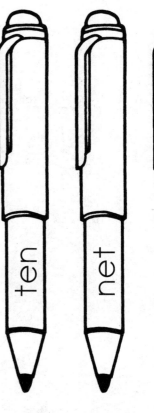

ten

net

tan

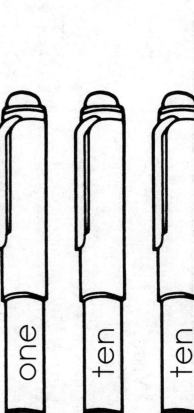

one

ten

ten

Name: _____

☆ 31 ☆
☆

11
eleven

Trace. Write.

eleven

Find each **11**. Color that space red. Then color the rest of the picture.

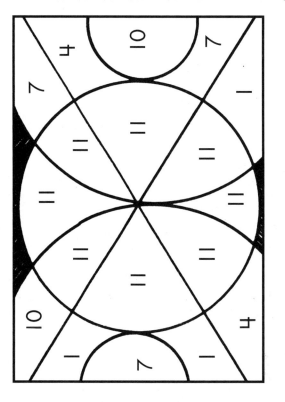

Circle each **11**.

9 11 7 11 2

5 11 10 4

Name: _____

32

Color **11** balls.

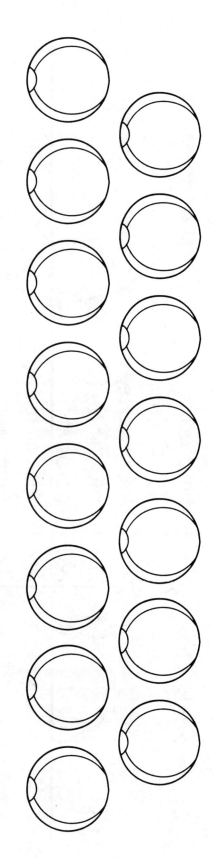

How many balls? Write the number in the box.

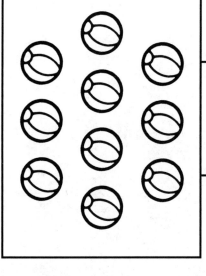

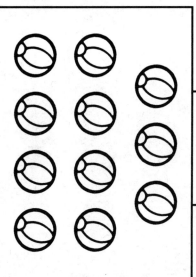

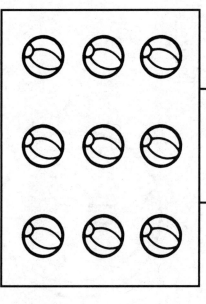

Name: _____

12
twelve

Trace. Write.

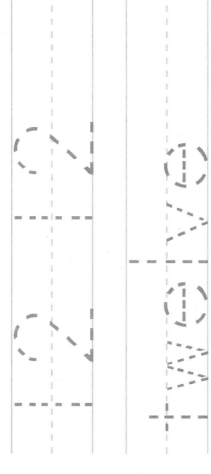

Circle each **12**.

12   4   12   1

2   10   7   11

12

Find each
12. Color
that space
pink. Then
color the
rest of the
picture.

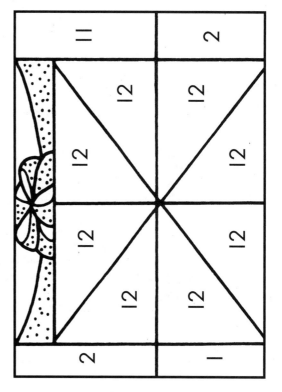

Name: _____

☆34 ☆
☆

Color **12** gifts.

How many gifts? Write the number in the box.

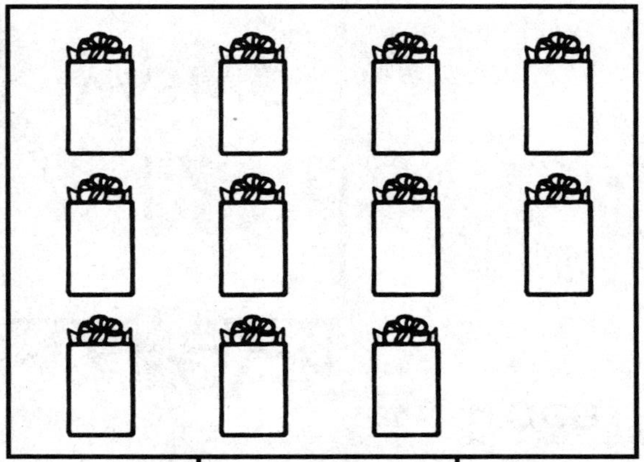

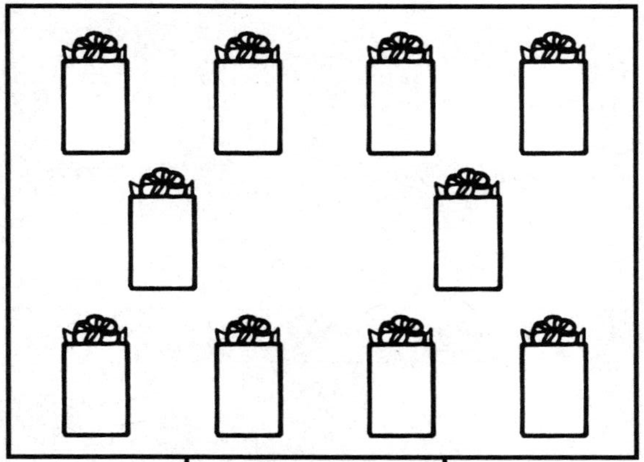

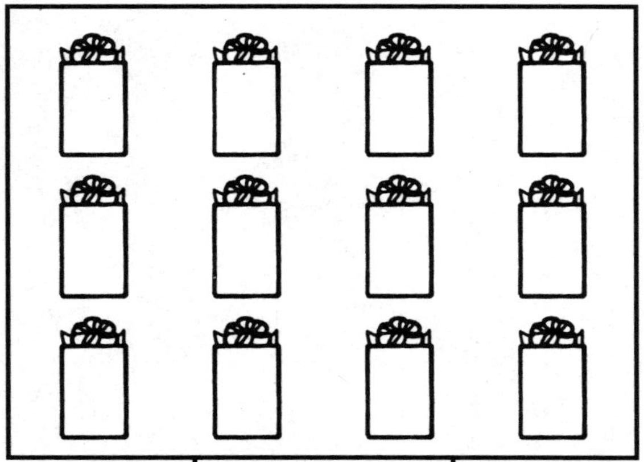

Name: _____

35

13
thirteen

Trace. Write.

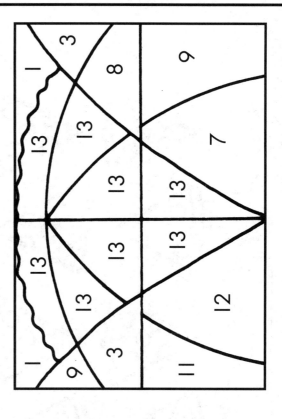

Find each
13. Color
that space
red. Then
color the
rest of the
picture.

Circle each 13.

3 8 13

13 11 13 1

13 12 10

Name: _____

Color **13** pizza slices.

How many pizza slices? Write the number in the box.

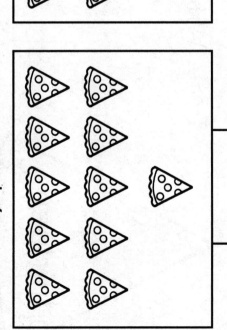

Name: _____

Trace. Write.

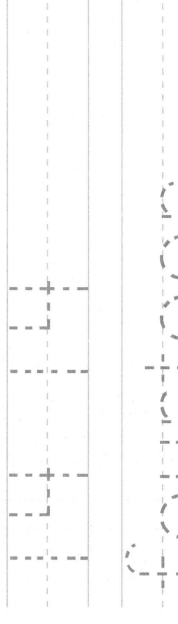

14
fourteen

Circle each **14**.

10   14   4   12

11   I   14

14   13

Find each
14. Color
that space
yellow.
Then color
the rest of
the picture.

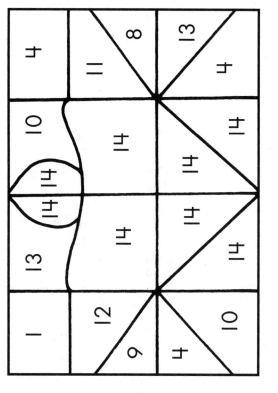

37

Name: _____

38

Color **14** candles.

How many candles? Write the number in the box.

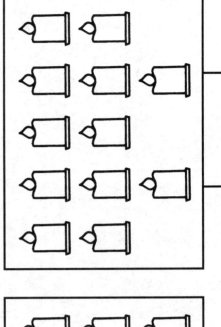

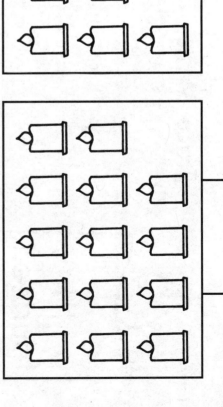

Name: _____

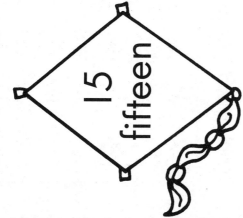

15
fifteen

Trace. Write.

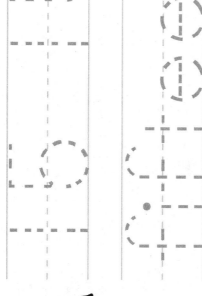

Circle each **15**.

5   15   I

    I2   15   I0

II   15   I4

Find each
15. Color
that space
purple.
Then color
the rest of
the picture.

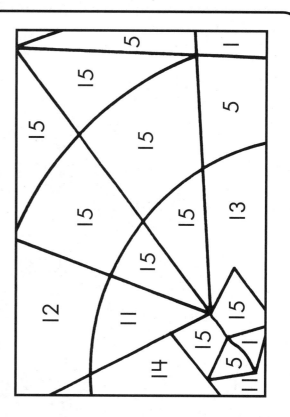

☆40 ☆☆ Name: _____

Color **15** kites.

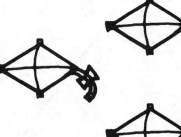
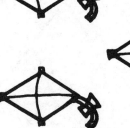

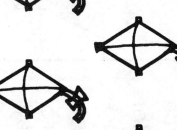

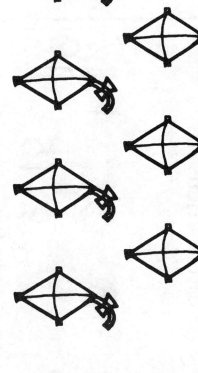

How many kites? Write the number in the box.

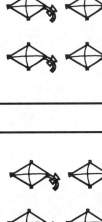

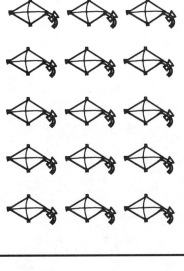

Name: _____

☆ 41 ☆
☆

Trace. Write.

16
sixteen

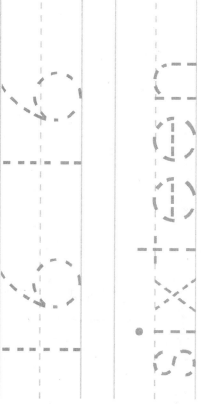

Circle each **16**.

10   1   9   16   16   12

16   8   16   6

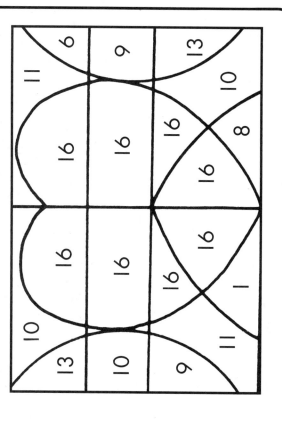

Find each **16**. Color that space red. Then color the rest of the picture.

42 ☆☆☆

Name: _____

Color **16** hearts.

How many hearts? Write the number in the box.

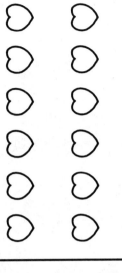

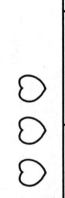

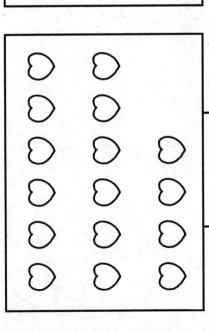

43

Name: _____

Trace. Write.

17

seventeen

seventeen

Circle each 17.

1   17   16   7   15

17   10   14   17

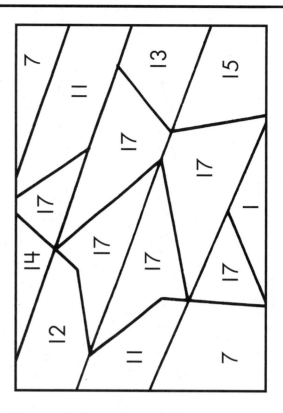

Find each
17. Color
that space
yellow.
Then color
the rest of
the picture.

7   11   13   15

17   17

14   17   17   1

12   17   17   17

11   7

44

Name: _____

Color **17** stars.

How many stars? Write the number in the box.

45

Name: _____

Trace. Write.

18
eighteen

18
eighteen

Circle each **18**.

15 1 18 16 8

18 10 12 18

Find each
18. Color
that space
green.
Then color
the rest of
the picture.

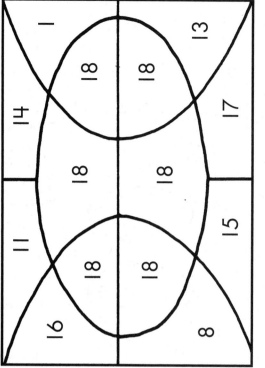

46

Name: _____

Color **18** ovals.

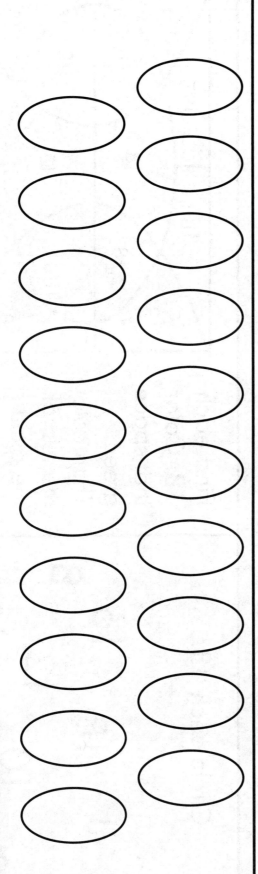

How many ovals? Write the number in the box.

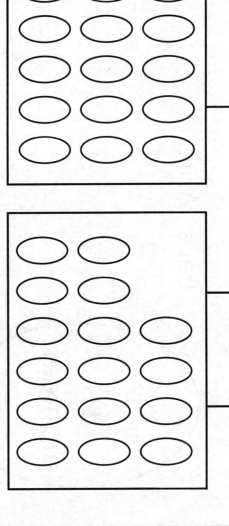

47 ☆

Name: _____

Trace. Write.

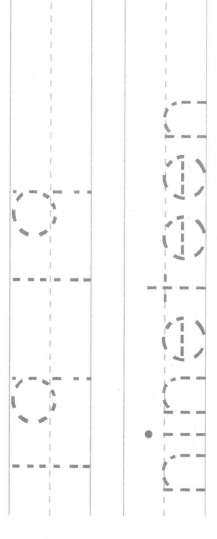

19
nineteen

nineteen

Find each **19**. Color that space red. Then color the rest of the picture.

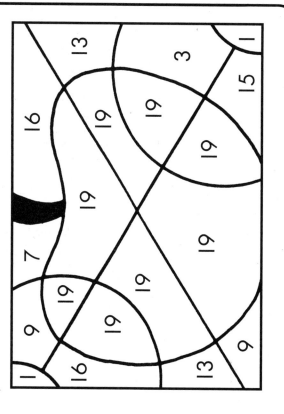

Circle each **19**.

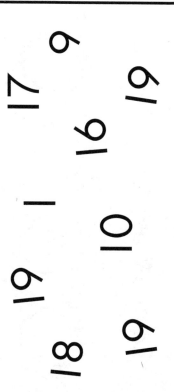

19   I   17   9

18   10   16   19

19

☆
48
☆☆

Name: _____

Color **19** apples.

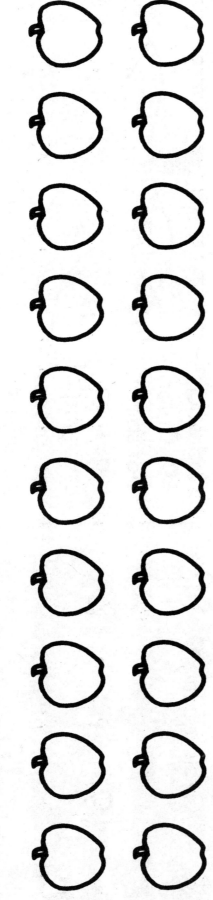

How many apples? Write the number in the box.

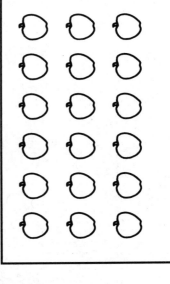

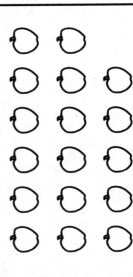

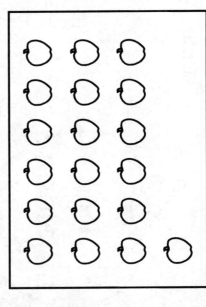

Name: _____

Trace. Write.

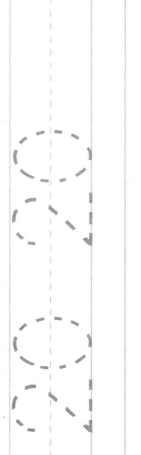

20
twenty

Circle each **20**.

12   2   20   0   10   19
     17   0   20
20

Find each
20. Color
that space
green.
Then color
the rest of
the picture.

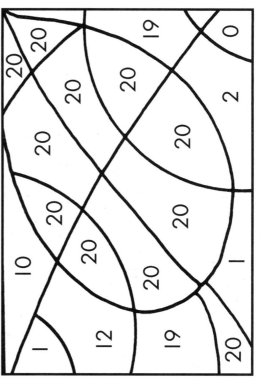

49

Name: _____

⭐50⭐

Color **20** leaves.

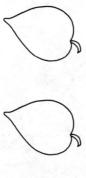

How many leaves? Write the number in the box.

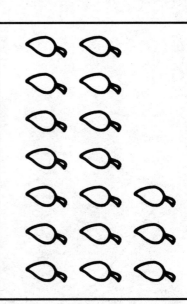

Name: _____

Trace. Write.

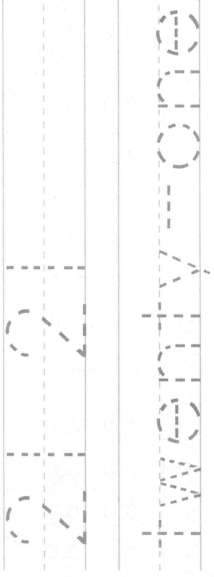

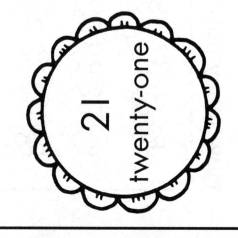

21
twenty-one

Circle each **21**.

12 21 10 19 11

22 21 21 20 21

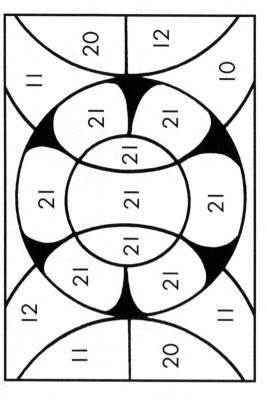

Find each
21. Color
that space
orange.
Then color
the rest of
the picture.

Name: _____

Color **21** flowers.

How many flowers? Write the number in the box.

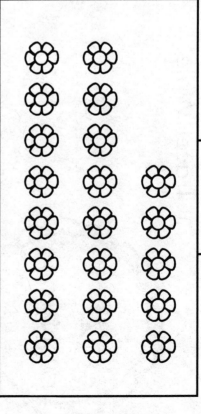

Name: _____

Trace. Write.

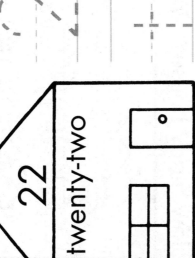

22

twenty-two

Circle each **22**.

22   10   22   21   2

20   12   15   22

Find each **22**. Color that space brown. Then color the rest of the picture.

21	18	15	2
12	22	22	17
19	22	22	22
	22	22	22	20

53

54

Name: _____

Color **22** houses.

How many houses? Write the number in the box.

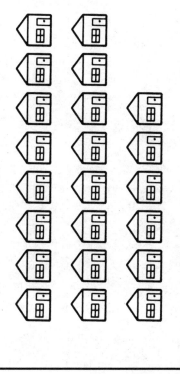

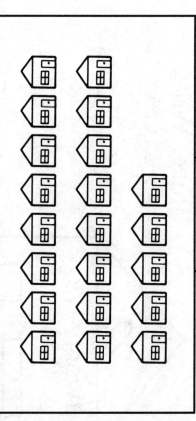

Name: _____

☆ 55 ☆☆

23
twenty-three

Trace. Write.

23 23

twenty-three

Find each
23. Color
that space
brown.
Then color
the rest of
the picture.

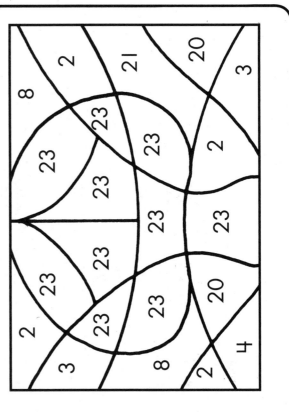

Circle each **23**.

23   8   13   23   2

20   3   23   18

Name: _____

☆56☆

Color **23** mushrooms.

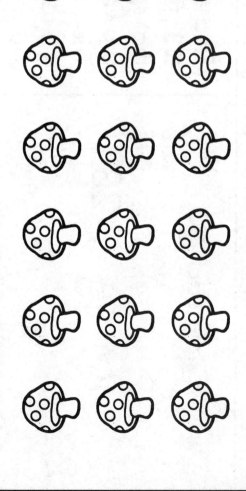

How many mushrooms? Write the number in the box.

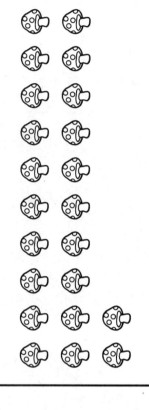

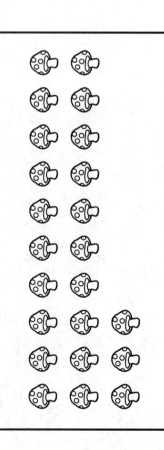

57 ⭐

Name: _____

Trace. Write.

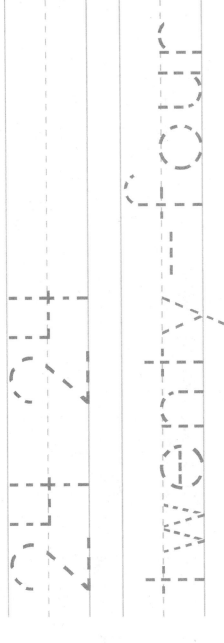

24
twenty-four

Find each
24. Color
that space
purple.
Then color
the rest of
the picture.

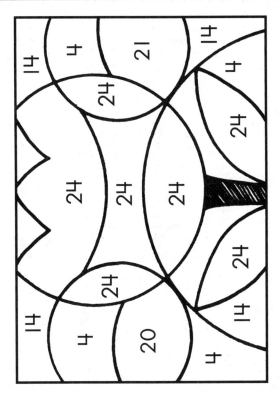

Circle each **24**.

21 22 24 13 12
    14 20 24
24

58

Name: _____

Color **24** flowers.

How many flowers? Write the number in the box.

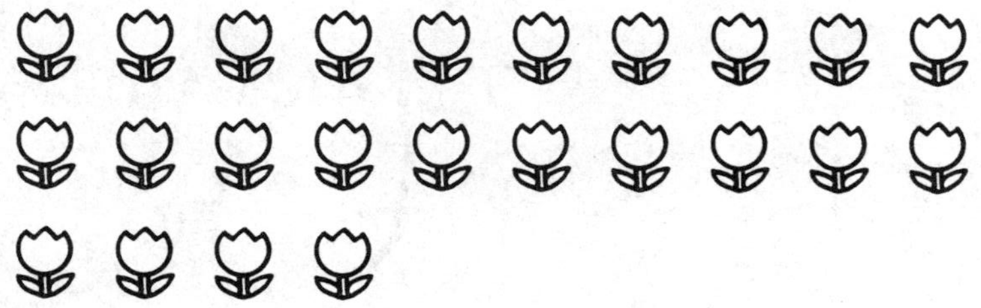

Name: _____

⭐ 59
⭐⭐

25
twenty-five

Trace. Write.

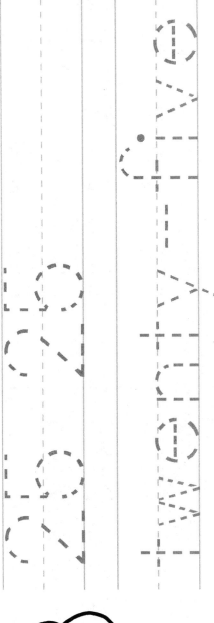

twenty-five

Circle each **25**.

23 25 20 15

5   25 25 22

24

Find each
25. Color
that space
green.
Then color
the rest of
the picture.

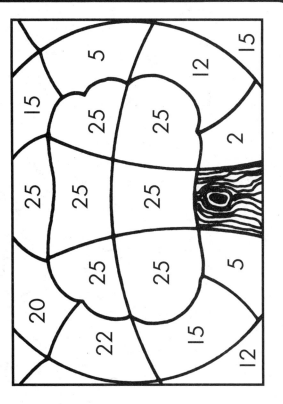

Name: _____

Color **25** trees.

How many trees? Write the number in the box.

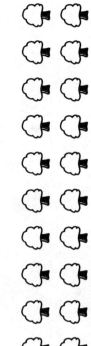

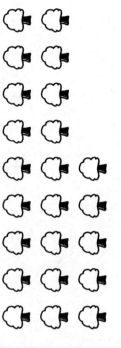

Name: _____

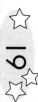
61

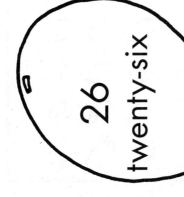

26
twenty-six

Trace. Write.

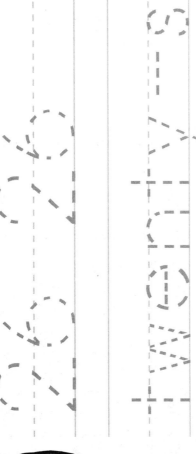

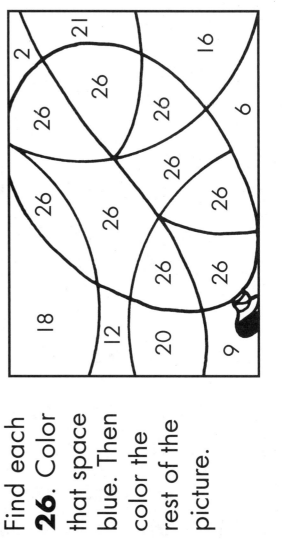

2	21
26	16
26	26
26	6
26	26
18	26
12	26
20	26
9

Find each **26**. Color that space blue. Then color the rest of the picture.

Circle each **26**.

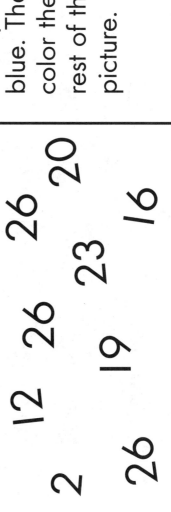

12   26   26   20

19   23

2   16

26

Name: _____

Color **26** balloons.

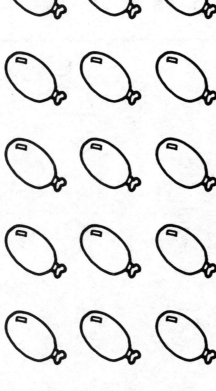

How many balloons? Write the number in the box.

Name: _____

27
twenty-seven

Trace. Write.

twenty-seven

Circle each **27**.

26 27 7 20 22

12 27 17 27

Find each **27**. Color that space red. Then color the rest of the picture.

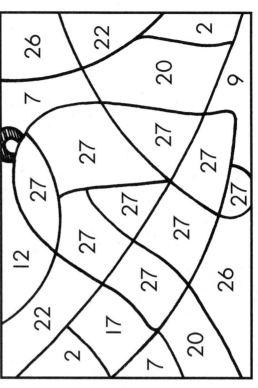

Name: _____

Color **27** bells.

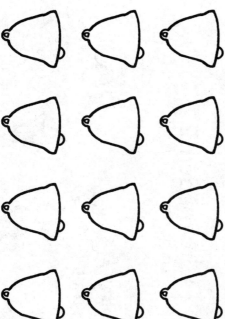

How many bells? Write the number in the box.

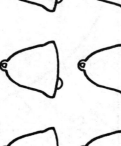

Name: _____

 65

28
twenty-eight

Trace. Write.

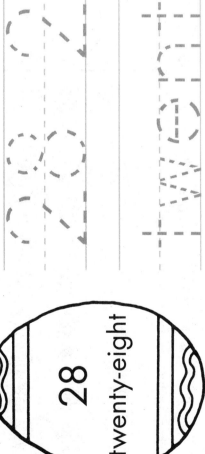

28 28

twenty-eight

Circle each **28**.

23 28 8 28 **13**

18

20 28 26

Find each
28. Color
that space
purple.
Then color
the rest of
the picture.

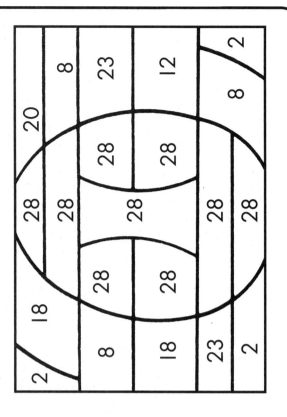

Name: _____

☆
☆☆ 66

Color **28** eggs.

How many eggs? Write the number in the box.

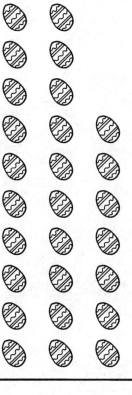

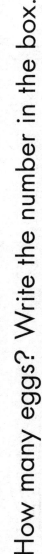

Name: _____

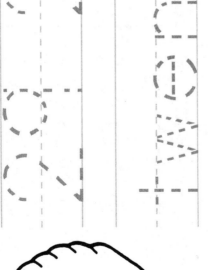

29
twenty-nine

Trace. Write.

29 29

twenty-nine

Find each **29**. Color that space pink. Then color the rest of the picture.

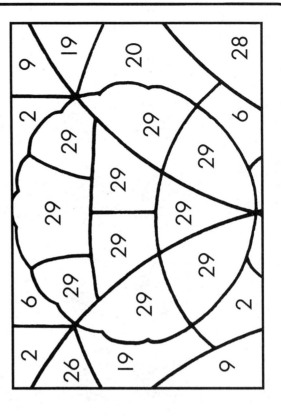

Circle each **29**.

29 20 16 29

18 9 19

29 26 29

Name: _____

Color **29** shells.

How many shells? Write the number in the box.

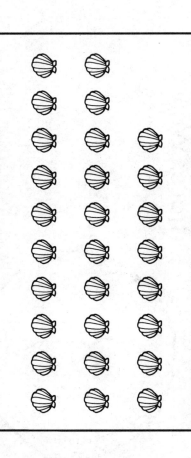

Name: _____

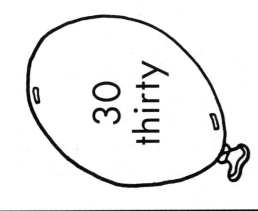

30
thirty

Trace. Write.

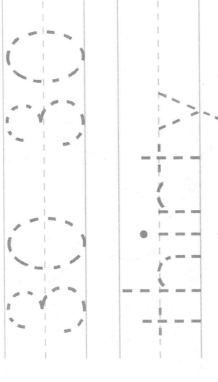

thirty

Circle each **30**.

13   30   20   10   3

30   23   2   30

Find each
30. Color
that space
blue. Then
color the
rest of the
picture.

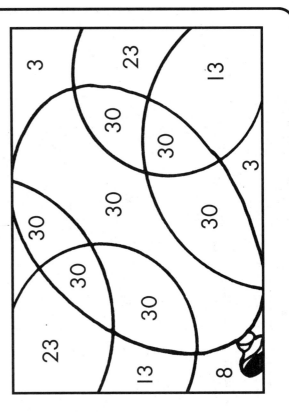

Name: _____

Color **30** balloons.

Connect the dots. Start at 19.

19

30

20

29

28

27

26

21

22

23

24

25

Name: _____

Trace. Write.

40
forty

Circle each **40**.

40   14   34   10

24   4

30   40   40

Find each **40**. Color that space pink. Then color the rest of the picture.

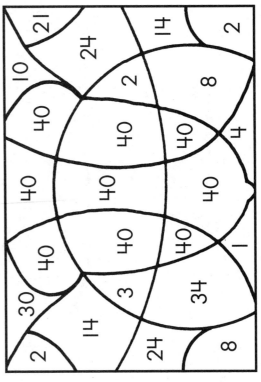

71

Connect the dots. Start at 30.

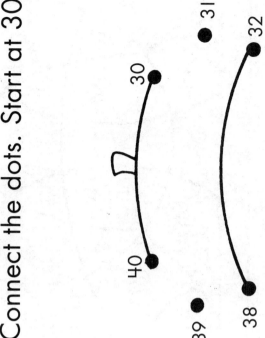
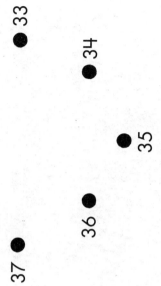

30
31
32
33
34
35
36
37
38
39
40

Name: _____

Color **40** acorns.

☆ 73 ☆☆

Name: _____

Trace. Write.

50

fifty

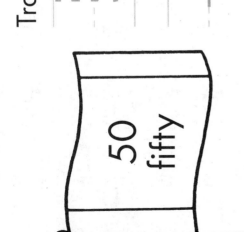

Circle each **50**.

20   50   45   25

35   50   5   50

15   50

Find each **50**. Color that space blue. Then color the rest of the picture.

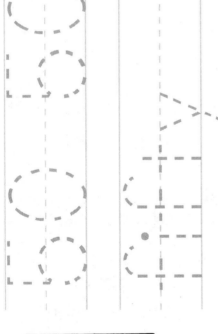

			4
50	50	30	50
50	50		1
50	50		50
50	50		5
15	50	2	
1			

Name: _____

Connect the dots. Start at 40.

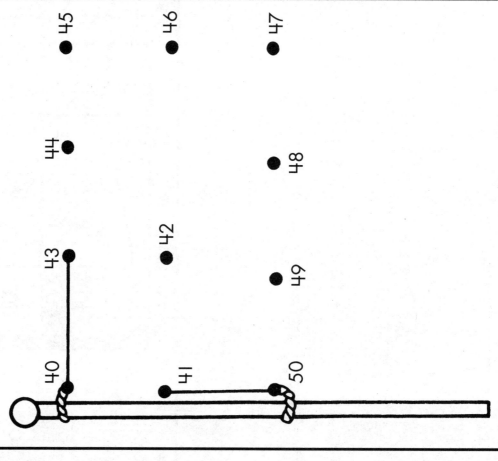

Color **50** flags.

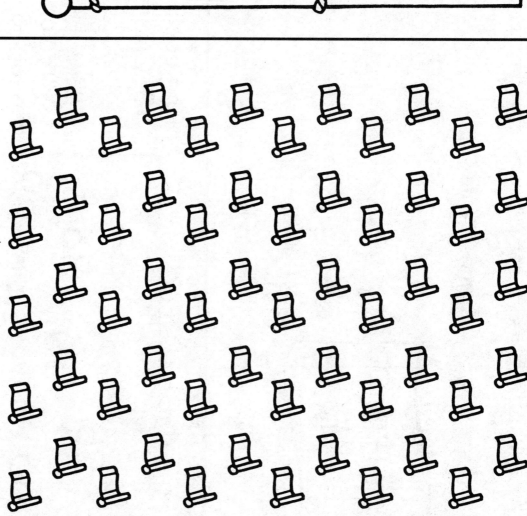

Name: _____

Trace. Write.

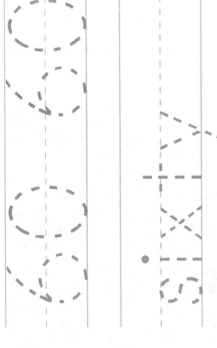

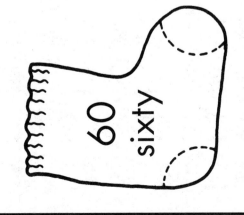

60
sixty

Find each **60**. Color that space brown. Then color the rest of the picture.

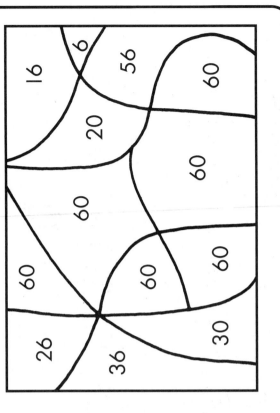

16		6
	20	56
		60
60	60	
60	60	60
26		30
	36	

Circle each **60**.

56   46   36   60

60   6   60

16   20

Connect the dots. Start at 50.

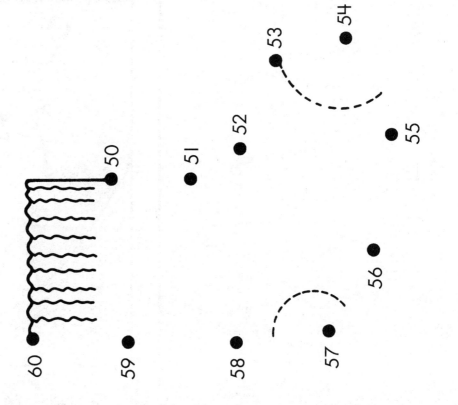

50
51
52
53
54
55
56
57
58
59
60

Name: _____

Color **60** socks.

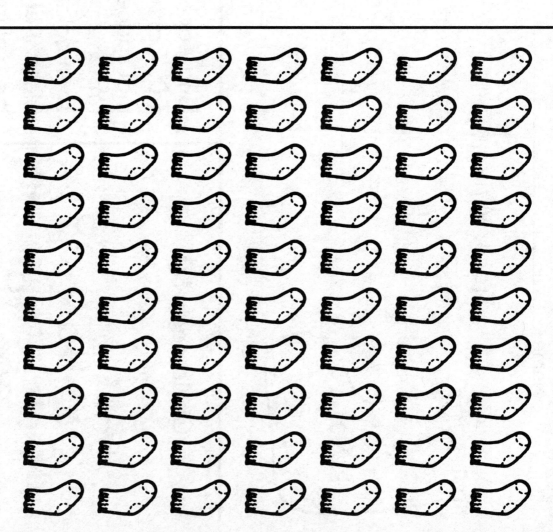

Name: _____

70
seventy

Trace. Write.

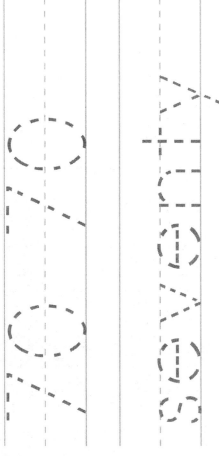

Find each **70**. Color that space red. Then color the rest of the picture.

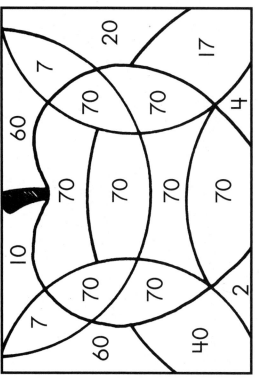

Circle each **70**.

7   57   70   20

17   47   70

40

Name: _____

Connect the dots. Start at 60.

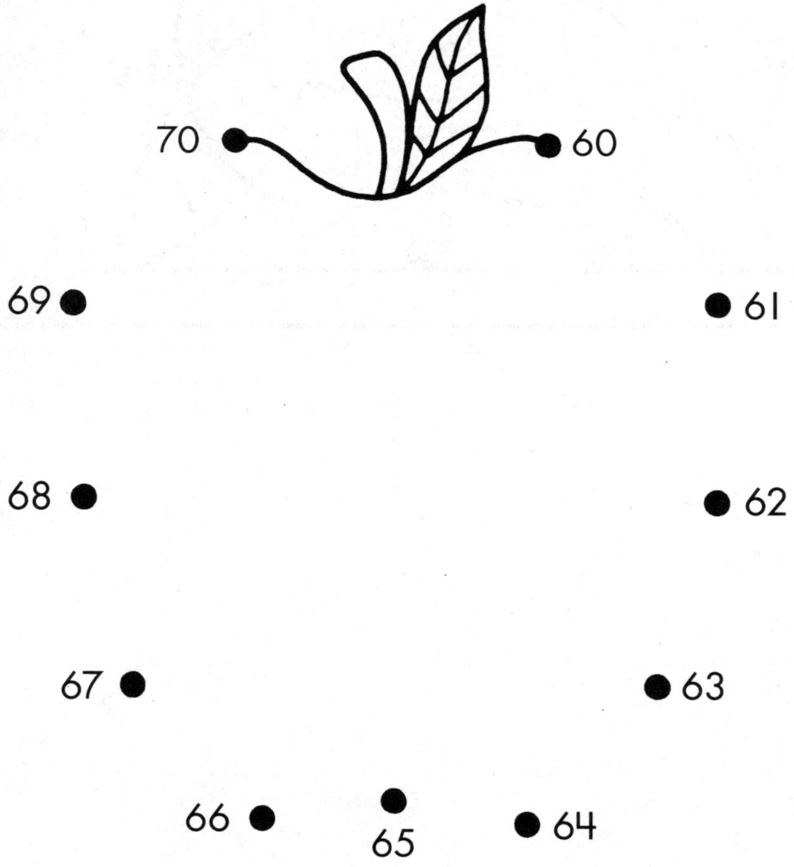

60
61
62
63
64
65
66
67
68
69
70

Color **70** apples.

Name: _____

79

80
eighty

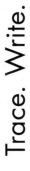

Trace. Write.

eighty

Circle each **80**.

80   18   68   30

8   38   80   60

80

Find each
80. Color
that space
orange.
Then color
the rest of
the picture.

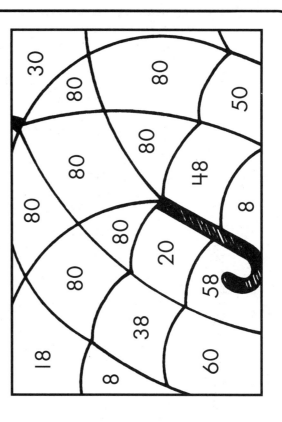

30	80	80		
80		80	80	
80	80		48	50
80		80		8
18	80	20	58	
	38	8	60	

Name: _____

80

Color **80** raindrops.

Connect the dots. Start at 70.

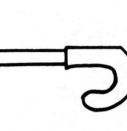

70
71
72
73
74
75
76
77
78
79
80

Name: _____

90
ninety

Trace. Write.

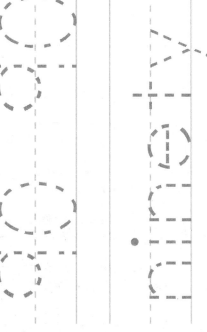

Circle each **90**.

9   19   90   89

70   60   90

39   90

Find each
90. Color
that space
green.
Then color
the rest of
the picture.

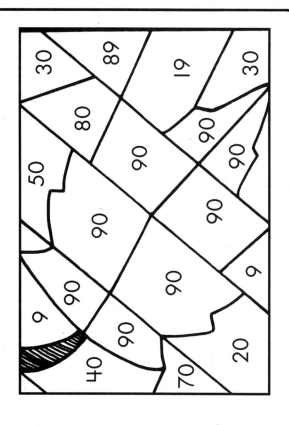

Connect the dots. Start at 80.

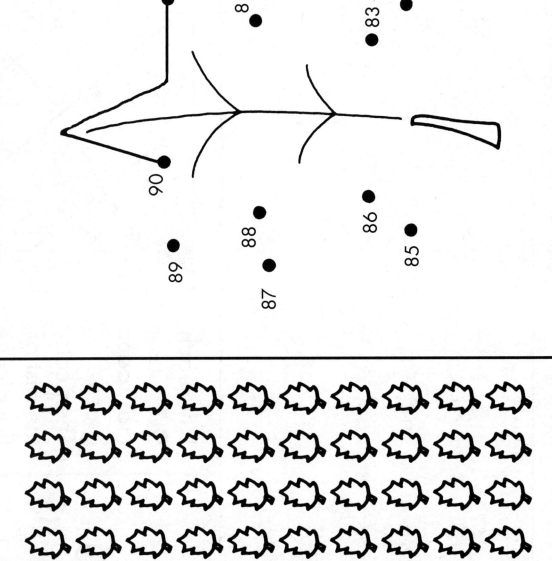

Name: _____

☆ 82 ☆☆

Color **90** leaves.

Name: _____

83

100

one hundred

Trace.

Circle each **100**.

100 10 80 17
11 1
70 100
100

Find each
100. Color
that space
yellow.
Then color
the rest of
the picture.

90	1	
11	10	0
	100	100
100		40
80	100	100
60	100	70
7	11	

Name: _____

Color **100** stars.

Connect the dots. Start at 91.

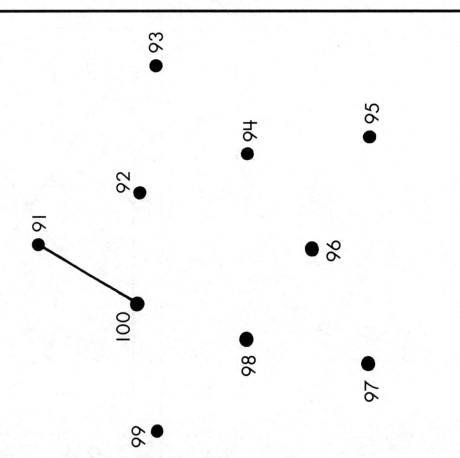

Name: _____

Write the missing numbers in each row. Color the **even** numbers.

Name: _____

86

Write the missing numbers in each row. Color the **even** numbers.

30		32	33		35
51			54		56
82		84		86	

Name: _____

Write the missing numbers in each row. Color the **odd** numbers.

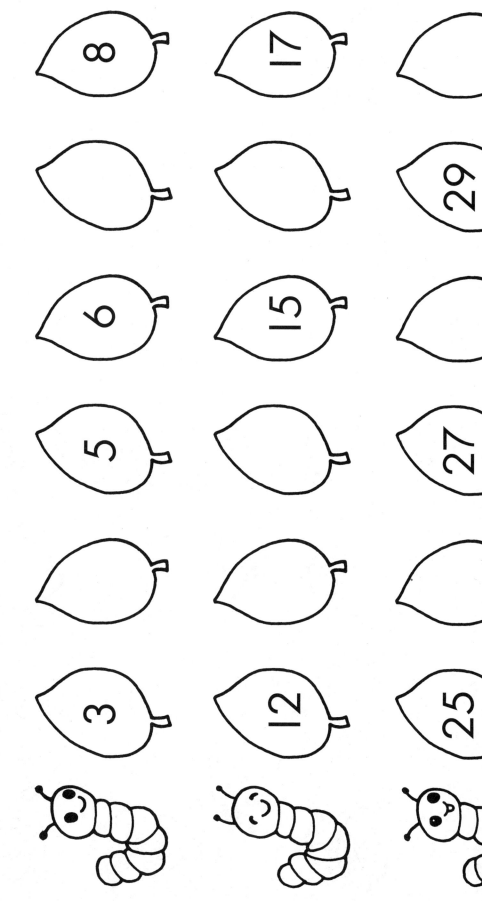

3		5	6		8
12			15		17
25		27		29	

87

Name: _____

Write the missing numbers in each row. Color the **odd** numbers.

40		42	43		45
72			75		77
93		95		97	

Now I Know My Numbers Learning Mats © 2012 Scholastic Teaching Resources • page 96

88

☆☆ 89
☆

Name: _____

Count the flowers in each set. Write the number in the box.

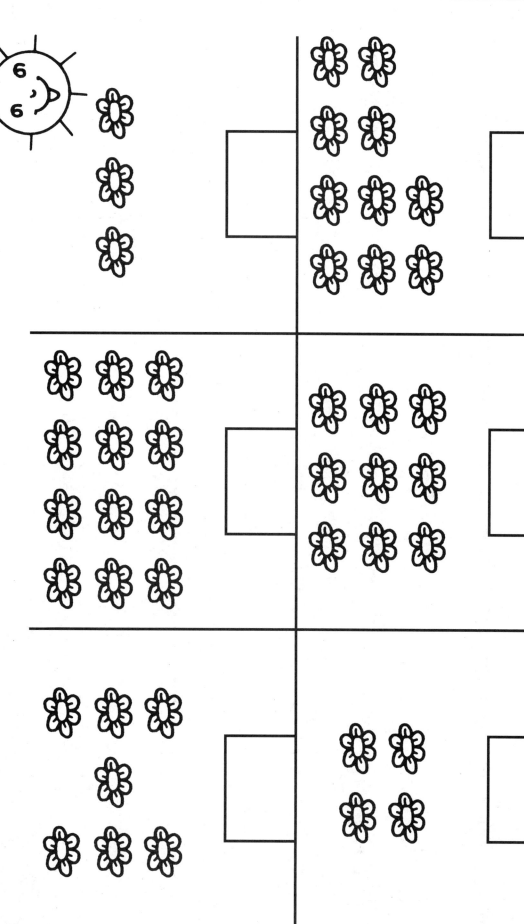

Name: _____

Count the eggs in each set. Write the number in the box.

Name: _____

Count the raindrops in each set. Write the number in the box.

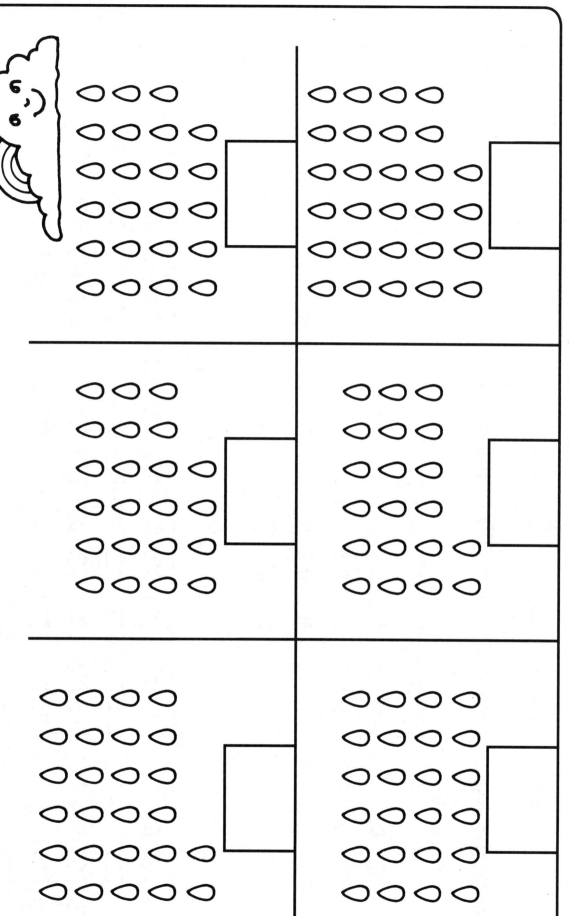

☆ 92 ☆

Name: _____

Count the fish in each set. Write the number in the box.

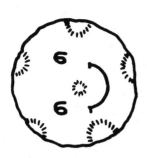

93

Name: _____

Count the stars in each set. Write the number in the box.

Name: _____

94

Count the apples in each set. Write the number in the box.

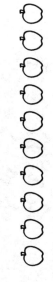

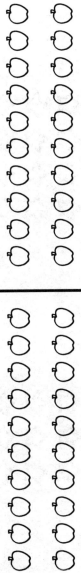

Name: _____

Compare the sets in each pair. Color the set that has **more**.

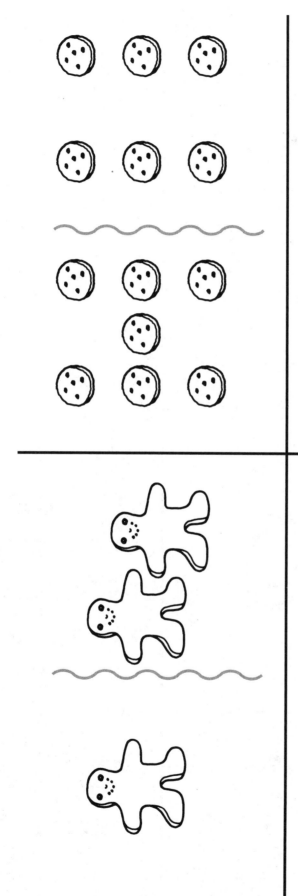

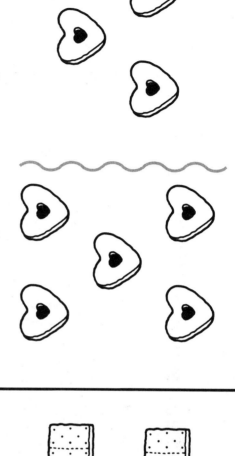

Name: _____

96

Compare the sets in each pair. Color the set that has **more**.

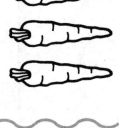

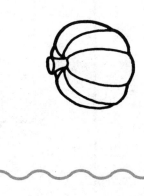

Name: _____

Compare the sets in each pair. Color the set that has **fewer**.

Now I Know My Numbers Learning Mats © 2012 Scholastic Teaching Resources • page 105

97

Name: _____

Compare the sets in each pair. Color the set that has **fewer**.

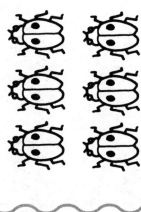

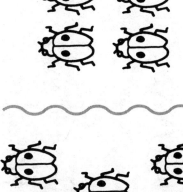
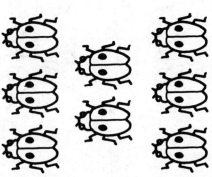
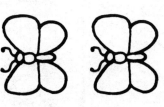

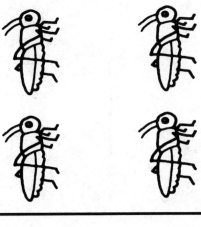
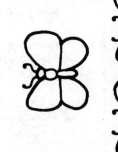

98

Name: _____

99

Match each number to its word.

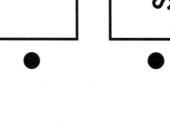

1 •   • two

2 •   • one

3 •   • four

4 •   • three

5 •   • six

6 •   • seven

7 •   • five

8 •   • eight

Name: _____

Match each number to its word.

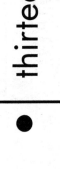 ●

nine ●

● 9

 ●

eleven ●

● 10

twelve ●

● 11

ten ●

● 12

---

fourteen ●

● 13

thirteen ●

● 14

sixteen ●

● 15

fifteen ●

● 16

Name: _____

Matching Numbers and Number Words

Match each number to its word.

17 ●	● twenty	● twenty-four
18 ●	● nineteen	● twenty-two
19 ●	● eighteen	● twenty-one
20 ●	● seventeen	● twenty-three

21 ●	
22 ●	
23 ●	
24 ●	

Name: _____

Match each number to its word.

102

30	•	forty
40	•	fifty
50	•	sixty
60	•	thirty

70	•	eighty
80	•	seventy
90	•	one hundred
100	•	ninety

☆103☆

Name: _____

Write the missing numbers to complete the chart.

									10
11									20
21									30
31									40
41									50

☆ 104 ☆

Name: _____

Write the missing numbers to complete the chart.

51									60
61									70
71									80
81									90
91									100